W9-BCO-490

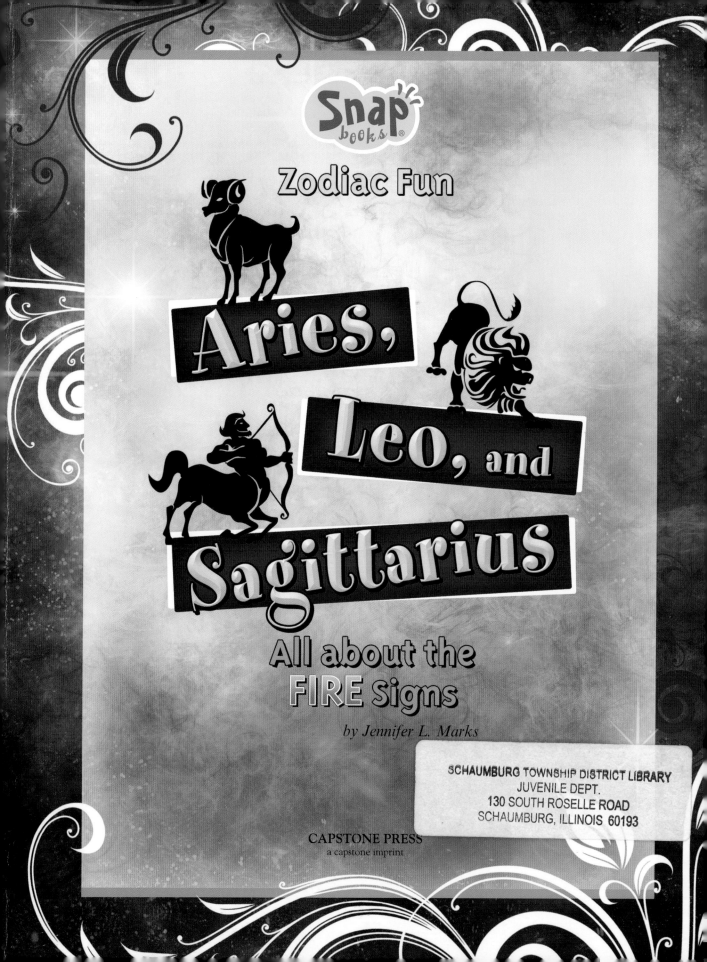

Snap books ®

Zodiac Fun

Aries, Leo, and Sagittarius

All about the FIRE Signs

by Jennifer L. Marks

CAPSTONE PRESS
a capstone imprint

Snap Books are published by Capstone Press,
151 Good Counsel Drive, P.O. Box 669, Mankato, Minnesota 56002.
www.capstonepress.com

092009
005618CGS10

Books published by Capstone Press are manufactured with paper
containing at least 10 percent post-consumer waste.

Library of Congress Cataloging-in-Publication Data
Marks, Jennifer, 1979–
     Aries, Leo, and Sagittarius : all about the fire signs / by Jennifer L. Marks.
     p. cm. — (Snap. Zodiac fun)
     Summary: "Provides information about the fire signs of the zodiac" — Provided by publisher.
     Includes bibliographical references and index.
     ISBN 978-1-4296-4014-5 (library binding)
     1. Aries (Astrology) — Juvenile literature. 2. Leo (Astrology) — Juvenile literature. 3. Sagittarius (Astrology) —
Juvenile literature. 4. Zodiac — Juvenile literature. I. Title. II. Series.
BF1727.M37 2010
133.5'2 — dc22   2009029189

Editor: Katy Kudela
Designer: Juliette Peters
Media Researcher: Jo Miller
Production Specialist: Laura Manthe

Photo Credits:
Capstone Studio/Karon Dubke, 32; Courtesy of the White House/Pete Souza, 20; Dreamstime/Terex, 24 (top right);
Getty Images Inc./FilmMagic/Jon Kopaloff, 27; Getty Images Inc./WireImage/Jeffrey Mayer, 13; iStockphoto/Mountain
Trails Photography, 23 (bottom right); NASA, 9 (bottom left); NASA/JPL/University of Arizona, 23 (bottom left);
Shutterstock/Alexandr Shebanov, 9 (bottom right); Shutterstock/arenacreative, 17 (bottom); Shutterstock/Baloncici, 4
(top left); Shutterstock/Danylchenko Iaroslav, 10 (top right); Shutterstock/Eugene Berman, 10 (bottom); Shutterstock/
Florian Andronache, 16 (top); Shutterstock/John Carnemolla, 6; Shutterstock/juliengrondin, 5; Shutterstock/Kochneva
Tetyana, 16 (bottom right); Shutterstock/Madlen, 8; Shutterstock/mujun, 24 (top left); Shutterstock/Okssi, 17 (top left);
Shutterstock/Pakhnyushcha, 12; Shutterstock/pdesign, 7 (bottom), 14 (bottom), 21 (bottom); Shutterstock/Peter Betts,
19; Shutterstock/pixshots, 24 (bottom); Shutterstock/Stephen Coburn, 26; Shutterstock/Sven Hoppe, 11; Shutterstock/
terehov igor, 17 (top right); Shutterstock/Tracy Whiteside, 18; Shutterstock/Triff, 15; Shutterstock/ulisse, 7 (top),
14 (top), 21 (top); Shutterstock/Wendy Nero, 9 (top); Shutterstock/wen mingming, 10 (top left); Shutterstock/Xsandra,
23 (top); Shutterstock/Ying Geng, 25; Shutterstock/YuliaPodlesnova, 22; SOHO, 16 (bottom left)

Design Elements
Shutterstock/argus; Shutterstock/Cihan Demirok; Shutterstock/Epic Stock; Shutterstock/Louisanne; Shutterstock/
Mikhail; Shutterstock/pdesign; Shutterstock/Rashevska Nataliia; Shutterstock/sabri deniz kizil; Shutterstock/solos

Essential content terms are `bold` and are defined at the bottom of the page where they first appear.

The author dedicates this book to Beth, her favorite Aries, and to Aaron — she thanks her lucky stars for him!

Table of Contents

Reading the Stars

You've probably browsed the **horoscope** column in the back of your favorite magazine. Ever wonder if that stuff is for real? There is no scientific proof that stars and planets affect personalities. Has that stopped people from believing in astrology? No way. Even though there's no real explanation, it can be fun to see what astrology says about you.

Basic astrology is simple. You won't need a map of the stars, a psychic friend, or the Magic 8-ball you stole from your brother's room. All you need to know is the position of the sun at the time of your birth. In other words, if you know your birthday, you can figure out your sign. It's just that easy.

In astrology, there are 12 signs of the zodiac. Astrologers group the signs into four elements — fire, air, earth, and water. Each element has three signs. Glowing bright under the fire sign are Aries, Leo, and Sagittarius. Take a closer look, and you'll see how fire and its three signs share a unique set of **traits**.

horoscope — a reading of the position of the stars and planets and how they might affect a person's life

trait — a characteristic that makes a person stand out from others

It's Elemental!

Bright, bold, and social, the fire signs are not afraid of stepping out and making a scene. They love living large. And why shouldn't they? After all, the fire signs are well-suited for life in the limelight.

How do fire signs mix with other elements?

Fire + Water

Ever cook a pot of spaghetti? If so, you'll know why fire and water can be a tricky combo. At best, water signs help fire signs cool off and relax. Fire signs liven up the dreamy water signs. At worst, these signs disagree and everything boils over.

Fire + Earth

Fire's need for excitement just might clash with earth's cautiousness. Still, this combo can be a solid pair. Fire signs help earth signs try something new. Earth keeps fire from rushing into bad choices.

Fire + Air

If the fire signs could choose sidekicks, it would be the air signs. Air fans the flames of fire's personality. And air signs really love the sassy attitude of fire signs. At worst, these two signs will be fierce, but respected, rivals.

Blazing a Trail

Aries, Leo, and Sagittarius are a red-hot trio of fun.
But there are slight differences between the three.
Here's a quick rundown of who's who in the sassy world of fire signs.

Aries
are independent trailblazers with tons of courage.

Leos
are social cats who love being the center of attention.

Sagittarians
are deep thinkers who like nothing more than the mysteries of life.

Want to learn more?

Keep reading to get the hot details on each sign.

If your birthday falls
March 21 through April 19,
your sign is

Aries

A Bold Sign

The Aries glyph looks like a Y. With a little imagination, you can make out a ram's head with horns.

Charging Ahead

Scaling a mountain? No problem. Aries' sign is the ram. Like a ram, Aries are no-nonsense achievers who reach great heights in whatever tasks they tackle.

glyph — a symbolic character

Personality Profile:
The Sizzle of an Aries

● Bold, confident, and talented, Aries love to be noticed.

● An Aries won't waste a minute fretting about mistakes or setbacks.

● Always positive, Aries can look on the bright side of any situation.

● Aries charge headfirst into any situation. They're not scared by the unknown.

What Makes an Aries Tick?

The saying "failure is not an option" was probably coined by an Aries. Winning is a big deal. Dig a little deeper, and you'll see that Aries really want to impress. People born under this sign secretly fear that others won't appreciate them. Worse, they fear people won't like them despite their oodles of trophies and awards.

Personality Minuses

careless with details
impatient
impulsive
short-tempered
stubborn

Personality Pluses

brave
energetic
honest
independent
positive

Just the Facts about Aries

Lucky day of week: Tuesday

Part of body ruled: head

Ruling planet: Mars

Flower: geranium

Fashion Trends

Aries want to be taken seriously. You won't find an Aries in a frilly sundress. Aries' style, in a word, is bold. The Aries' lucky color is daring red. Purple and black also make the list. Although they love solid colors, Aries wear plaids, stripes, and black-and-white combos. No matter the outfit, an Aries will never look sloppy.

An Aries' stone of choice is the diamond. After all, diamonds are this sign's lucky stone.

The Pro Ram

What is an Aries' dream job? Being the boss, of course. Careers in public relations, politics, training, sports, and the military are spot-on.

Active Social Life

How does an Aries' social life look? Competitive sports are a surefire hit with any Aries. This sign won't turn down a challenge. Who will an Aries pick for teammates?

BFFs

Aries like to be with positive and chatty signs. Naturally, an Aries will get along with other fire signs. Gemini and Aquarius are an Aries' faves too.

Not So Hot

Aries will avoid signs that spend too much time thinking and not enough time doing. Capricorn and Taurus are bound to wear down an Aries' patience.

Is an Aries Totally Crush-Worthy?

An Aries is quite the catch. If you love fun outings, this sign is definitely right for you. Don't be shy. An Aries loves a flirty and direct approach.

How to Spot Aries

- They look everyone directly in the eyes and have a hearty handshake.
- They aren't afraid to say exactly what they think.
- They dress to impress.
- They have a habit of talking back . . . even when they probably shouldn't.

It's All in the Stars:
Famous Aries

Maya Angelou

Fergie

America Ferrera

Kate Hudson

Thomas Jefferson

Nancy Pelosi

Kristen Stewart

Vincent van Gogh

Emma Watson

Reese Witherspoon

Kristen Stewart

Birthday: April 9, 1990

Kristen Stewart blazed a trail onto the big screen with her role as Bella Swan in *Twilight*. This talented Aries began acting at age 8. Always up for a challenge, this young star took on TV and movie roles. In 2002 Kristen made her name in Hollywood, and she's been booking film roles ever since. This sparkling Aries will continue tackling movie roles. She also has plans to go to college and may someday follow a writing career.

If your birthday falls
July 23 through August 22,
your sign is

Leo

A Sizzling Sign

The Leo glyph looks a little like a lion's mane. After all, Leo's animal of choice is the lion.

Happily Purring

Leos are fun-loving cats. They live to be liked. They easily steal the show at any gathering. Most of the time, a Leo is like a happy cat snoozing in the sun. But look out. A tiny sliver in those big lion paws can cause a fuss.

Personality Profile:

The Sizzle of a Leo

- These sociable cats easily make new friends.

- Leos' sunny attitude makes them super likeable.

- Leos have few enemies. They generally accept people for who they are.

- Leos are horrible at hiding their feelings. They wear their hearts on their sleeves.

What Makes a Leo Tick?

Leos go gaga for respect and attention. They like to win at anything because it earns them the approval they crave. But life isn't just a popularity contest. Leos want to love and be loved. Who could ask for more?

Personality Pluses

dignified
generous
honest
lively and upbeat
loyal

Personality Minuses

braggy
coldhearted when hurt
headstrong
stubborn
takes undue credit

Just the Facts about Leo

Parts of body ruled: back, spine, and heart

Ruling planet: Sun

Lucky day of week: Sunday

Flower: sunflower

Fashion Trends

Fiery red jackets, glittering gold bling, and leopard print shoes. You'll definitely know a Leo when you see one. When it comes to clothes, Leos love to be seen. Sleek, fitted outfits, trendy sunglasses, and designer brands are all Leo faves. These fashionable felines strive to look classy. But they like comfort too. Dressed like a comfy kitten or a stylin' lion, Leos always look amazing.

Leos will shine with gold jewelry. Throw a ruby into the mix, and a Leo will have plenty of good luck.

The Pro Leo

A Leo craves jobs in the public eye. Politics and public relations are good careers. Sales jobs are another match. For the friendly lion, a career in entertainment is another primo option.

A Leo's Social Scene

Leos adore being in the limelight. They want to live the dream and be with others who do the same. How does a Leo's social life shake out?

BFFs

Leos understand each other best. But Leos also get along well with other upbeat and loving signs. Who makes for a super close pal? Leos pair well with Aries, Gemini, and Cancer. They also match up with Libra and Sagittarius.

Not So Hot

It's no surprise that Leos don't have time for a Taurus or a Virgo. These earth signs are simply too cautious for fiery Leos.

Could a Leo Make You Melt?

If you love to live it up, a Leo is prime crush material. Remember, a Leo is king of the jungle. You've got to dress to impress. Also, if you've traveled the globe, be sure to let your Leo crush know.

How to Spot Leos

• They have fabulous hair and like to fuss with it.
• Their heads are almost always held high.
• They are dressed to impress and look good in all situations.
• They speak in loud, strong voices.

It's All in the Stars:
Famous Leos

Neil Armstrong
Halle Berry
Bill Clinton
Amelia Earhart
Joe Jonas

Jennifer Lopez
President Barack Obama
Hayden Panettiere
Daniel Radcliffe
Charlize Theron

Barack Obama

Birthday: August 4, 1961

In 2008, Barack Obama's upbeat attitude received loads of voter support. A typical Leo, President Obama has a talent for reaching out to others. During his first few months in office, the president worked to improve U.S. relations with the world. The world quickly welcomed the president. As a positive Leo, President Obama is sure to have the continued support of others.

If your birthday falls
November 22 through December 21,
your sign is

Sagittarius

A Daring Sign

The Sagittarius glyph is easy to remember. It looks like an archer's arrow.

Taking Aim

The Sagittarius symbol is the archer. People also use the centaur to represent this sign. The centaur, half human and half horse, is a creature from **mythology**. Sagittarius is linked with horses and all kinds of pets.

mythology — a collection of myths

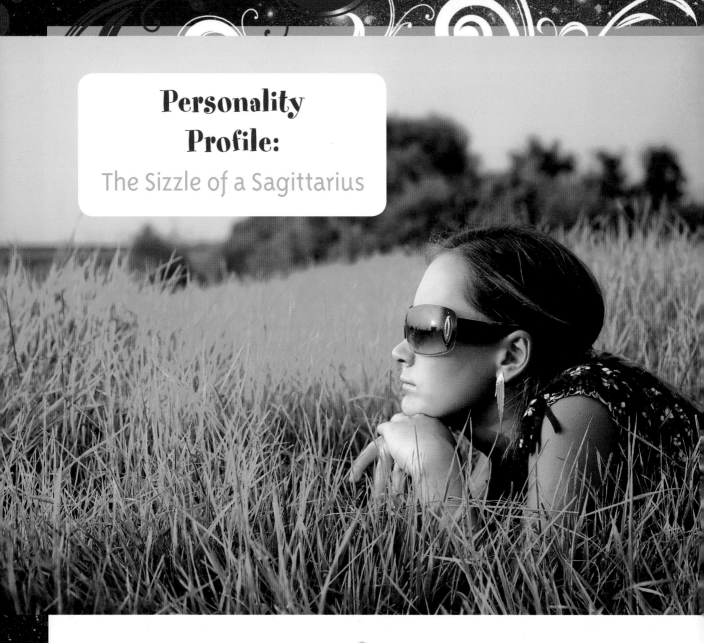

Personality Profile:
The Sizzle of a Sagittarius

- "To be, or not to be . . ." A deep thinker, a Sagittarius ponders life's big questions. Hmmm . . .

- At a party, a Sagittarius will turn on the charm. This sign is a true social butterfly.

- "Oops! Shouldn't have said that . . ." Brutally honest, a Sagittarius may say too much.

- Look the other way! It's often easier for a Sagittarius to ignore a problem than face it.

What Makes a Sagittarius Tick?

Sagittarians want to be free and happy. They want to be able to live life on their own terms. Rules drive Sagittarians bonkers. Also, they simply love people and dislike the idea that suffering is a part of life.

Personality Pluses

adventurous
cheerful
fair
fun
honest

Personality Minuses

has trouble sharing
impatient
poor planner
restless
short-tempered

Just the Facts about Sagittarius

Parts of body ruled: liver, hips, and thighs

Lucky day of week: Thursday

Flower: holly

Ruling planet: Jupiter

Fashion Trends

This fire sign is all about hassle-free fashion. A trusty pair of jeans, comfy boots, and a flowy top is perfect for the archer girl. Fussy clothes are not an option. Anything with too many buttons, hooks, snaps, or laces will drive a Sagittarius crazy. Cute but functional hoodies, canvas shoes, and flats are all mainstays in this sign's wardrobe. For a formal event, nothing suits a Sagittarius better than a fitted dress. A dramatic color, such as purple, fits this sign best.

Turquoise is a must-have item for this fire sign's wardrobe. This stone is said to bring a Sagittarius good luck.

The Pro Sagittarius

A Sagittarius that's on the job works fast and furious. This sign is a coworker fave. What's a Sagittarius career of choice? This fire sign likes jobs that require a lot of thinking and physical work. Look for careers in research, travel businesses, or veterinary sciences.

Social Sagittarius

Fab Sagittarians love playing extreme team sports and games of chance. They enjoy exploring foreign cultures and caring for animals. Who will a Sagittarius pick to join them on life's adventures?

BFFs

Sagittarians need friends that can keep up with them. They are best matched with an Aries, Leo, Libra, or Aquarius.

Not So Hot

Slow and steady Taurus and Virgo will have a hard time understanding a Sagittarius' love for constant movement.

Are You Crushin' on a Sagittarius?

A Sagittarius is a total heartthrob. If an archer has caught your eye, just be caring and casual. This fire sign will like your light-hearted attitude. Remember, a Sagittarius appreciates a good sense of humor too.

How to Spot Sagittarians

- They always carry their passports with them, just in case.
- They strike up conversations with strangers.
- They can't sit still. If you see a sitting Sagittarius, check for a furiously tapping toe or a wildly wiggling foot.
- LOL! They laugh at their own mistakes.

It's All in the Stars:
Famous Sagittarians

Tyra Banks   Scarlett Johansson
Miley Ray Cyrus   Brad Pitt
Walt Disney   Raven-Symoné
Jake Gyllenhaal   Steven Spielberg
Jay-Z   Mark Twain

Miley Ray Cyrus

Birthday: November 23, 1992

Singer, TV star, and actress, Miley Ray Cyrus is a fierce Sagittarius. Born and raised in Tennessee, this sparkling Sagittarius knew she wanted to follow her father's footsteps. Miley landed her first TV role at age 8. Miley's confidence kept her moving forward. At age 12, Miley landed the lead role on the hit Disney show *Hannah Montana*. Today Miley's star continues to shine on TV as well as on the big screen and concert stage.

Quiz: Are You In Your Element?

Are you a dreamy water girl, a feisty fire diva, an airy social butterfly, or a down-to-earth goddess? Find out which element describes you best by taking this quiz.

1. A girl in your math class invites you to a party. You don't know her well. You:
- Ⓐ thank her, but politely decline. You have plans to babysit.
- Ⓑ don't commit. Maybe you'll go if you feel like it that day.
- Ⓒ say yes, but you won't show. Your crew would never be caught there.
- Ⓓ agree, of course! You're sure to meet some cool people there.

2. The perfect date would be:
- Ⓐ dinner and a movie.
- Ⓑ a moonlit walk on the beach.
- Ⓒ deep conversation at an indie coffee shop.
- Ⓓ hanging out at the school dance.

3. There's a girls' night this Friday, and you:
- Ⓐ got elected to host the event.
- Ⓑ arrive late but bring the best snacks.
- Ⓒ will be the life of the party.
- Ⓓ would rather go on a date.

4. Your usual workout routine consists of:
- Ⓐ walking, hiking, jogging . . . put you on a trail and off you go.
- Ⓑ swimming laps either early or late when you have the pool mostly to yourself.
- Ⓒ you and your buddy teaming up at a gym.
- Ⓓ fast-pitch softball, basketball, or volleyball. Competitive sports are your thing.

5. You come down with the worst cold of the 21st century. You:
- Ⓐ stock up on cold medicine and keep on truckin'.
- Ⓑ whimper and request some TLC from family and friends.
- Ⓒ have your mom call you in sick. One day of rest never hurts.
- Ⓓ ignore it until it's absolutely unbearable.

6. It's Saturday night. You are:
- Ⓐ cooking a fave meal for a group of friends.
- Ⓑ rocking out at the nearest music concert.
- Ⓒ hard-core shopping.
- Ⓓ dancing the night away.

7. You're packing your lunch. These foods are on your menu:
- Ⓐ fresh, healthy food.
- Ⓑ comfort food.
- Ⓒ junk food, then diet food, then junk food.
- Ⓓ leftover takeout from the night before.

8. Your idea of a great night alone is:
- Ⓐ popcorn and an awesome book.
- Ⓑ a warm bubble bath and your fave chick flick.
- Ⓒ writing your latest philosophy on life.
- Ⓓ calling up friends.

9. Your favorite outfit is:
- Ⓐ low maintenance and looks great on you.
- Ⓑ whatever feels comfy.
- Ⓒ so trendy that it changes each week!
- Ⓓ stylish and sassy.

10. You just can't say no to:
- Ⓐ a friend in need.
- Ⓑ anything free.
- Ⓒ a social gathering.
- Ⓓ a challenge.

Zodiac Chart

Aries
March 21–April 19
Fire
- brave
- confident
- energetic

Leo
July 23–August 22
Fire
- dignified
- generous
- playful

Sagittarius
November 22–December 21
Fire
- adventurous
- cheerful
- fun

Taurus
April 20–May 20
Earth
- friendly
- loyal
- trustworthy

Virgo
August 23–September 22
Earth
- helpful
- observant
- practical

Capricorn
December 22–January 19
Earth
- determined
- hardworking
- wise

Gemini
May 21–June 20
Air
- clever
- curious
- lively

Libra
September 23–October 22
Air
- charming
- fair
- polite

Aquarius
January 20–February 18
Air
- daring
- honest
- independent

Cancer
June 21–July 22
Water
- caring
- gentle
- sensitive

Scorpio
October 23–November 21
Water
- confident
- fearless
- flirty

Pisces
February 19–March 20
Water
- artistic
- creative
- kind

Quiz Key

When scoring your answers, (A) equals 1 point, (B) equals 2 points, (C) equals 3 points, and (D) equals 4 points. Add them up to discover which element fits you best!

35–40 = You are social and love the spotlight. Are you an Aries, a Leo, or a Sagittarius? If not, the **fire** signs have had a strong effect on your personality.

26–34 = You definitely have a social agenda and plenty of ideas. Are you a Gemini, a Libra, or an Aquarius? If not, the **air** signs have had a strong effect on your personality.

16–25 = You are creative and emotional. Are you a Cancer, a Scorpio, or a Pisces? If not, the **water** signs have had a strong effect on your personality.

10–15 = You are realistic, practical, and grounded. Are you a Taurus, a Virgo, or a Capricorn? If not, the **earth** signs have had a strong effect on your personality.

Glossary

astrology (uh-STROL-uh-jee) — the study of how the positions of stars and planets affect people's lives

centaur (SEN-tor) — a creature that is half human and half horse

element (EL-uh-muhnt) — one of the four categories of signs found in the zodiac; the elements are air, earth, fire, and water.

glyph (GLIF) — a symbolic character; each of the 12 astrology signs has individual glyphs.

horoscope (HOR-uh-skope) — a reading of the position of the stars and planets and how they might affect a person's life

mythology (mi-THOL-uh-jee) — a collection of myths

trait (TRATE) — a quality or characteristic that makes one person different from another

unique (yoo-NEEK) — one of a kind

zodiac (ZOH-dee-ak) — the arrangement of signs that fill a year, beginning and ending in March

Read More

Aslan, Madalyn. *What's Your Sign? A Cosmic Guide for Young Astrologers.* New York: Grosset & Dunlap, 2002.

Hainer, Michelle. *DK Girl World Quiz Zone 2: 50 New Quizzes to Figure Out Your Friends and Forecast Your Future!* New York: Dorling Kindersley, 2007.

Jones, Jen. *Cancer, Scorpio, and Pisces: All about the Water Signs.* Zodiac Fun. Mankato, Minn.: Capstone Press, 2010.

Internet Sites

FactHound offers a safe, fun way to find Internet sites related to this book. All of the sites on FactHound have been researched by our staff.

Here's all you do:

Visit *www.facthound.com*

FactHound will fetch the best sites for you!

Index

About the Author

Jennifer L. Marks is a solar Virgo/lunar Scorpio. Astrology has fascinated her since she was old enough to own a library card. She works as an author and editor in Mankato, Minnesota, and has an MFA in creative writing. A true Virgo, Jennifer loves reading, researching, writing, editing, making to-do lists, cleaning, and taking care of her many pets. She is also an accomplished worrywart.